W9-AVN-288

Why hire **Roberto**?
Why hire **Katharine**?
Why hire **Mohammed**?
Why hire **Hannah**?
Why hire **Jordan**?
Why hire **Amanda**?
Why hire **Juanita**?
Why hire **David**?
Why hire **George**?
Why hire **Taylor**?
Why hire **Kanesha**?
Why hire **Laila**?
Why hire **Sarah**?
Why hire **Jamal**?
Why hire **Aaron**?
Why hire **Michele**?
Why hire **Jennifer**?

Why Hire Jennifer?

How to Use Branding
and Uncommon Sense
to Get Your First Job,
Last Job, and Every Job
in Between.

Richard W. Lewis

Also by Richard W. Lewis

ABSOLUT BOOK.

The Absolut Vodka Advertising Story.

ABSOLUT SEQUEL.

The Absolut Advertising Story Continues.

**Dedicated to Little Mom:
You Made Me Appreciate Words
and the Houses Where They Live**

Why Hire Jennifer?

How to Use Branding and Uncommon Sense to Get Your First Job,
Last Job, and Every Job in Between.

Richard W. Lewis

RL Ideas, Ltd.
256 Clinton Avenue
Dobbs Ferry, NY 10522

Printed by CreateSpace, An Amazon.com Company

More information at whyhirejennifer.com

To report errors, please send a note to rl@rlconsulting.biz

Copyright © 2014 by Richard W. Lewis

Book Designer: Juergen Dahlen

Notice of Rights.
All rights reserved. No part of this book may be reproduced or transmitted in any form by any means. Electronic, mechanical, photocopying, recording, or otherwise, without the prior written permission of the author. For information on getting permission for reprints and excerpts contact rl@rlconsulting.biz

Notice of liability.
The information in this book is distributed on an "as is" basis without warranty. While every precaution has been taken in the preparation of the book, the author shall have no liability to any person or entity with respect to any loss or damage caused or alleged to be caused directly or indirectly by the instructions contained in this book.

Trademarks.
Many of the designations used by manufacturers and sellers to distinguish their products are claimed as trademarks. All product names and services identified throughout this book are used in editorial fashion only and for the benefit of such companies with no intention of infringement of the trademark. No such use, or the use of any trade name, is intended to convey endorsement or other affiliation with this book.

ISBN 978-1499199871

Printed and bound in the United States of America.

**"The Way We Do Anything
is the Way We Do Everything."**

-- Martha Beck

Table of Contents

Introduction.

I'll keep this short. I've learned from my advertising life that people only read what they want to read.

I've learned from my college professor life that students will not read anything they aren't required to read.

Introductions fall into both categories.

As a writer I prefer you read this book sequentially: Beginning to middle to end.

My job and career hunting advice uses building blocks.

But if you're not wired to learn like that, don't worry about it. You will still learn lots of useful stuff here if all you do is inhale, jump around, and inhale some more.

The designer, Juergen Dahlen, and I intentionally made **Why Hire Jennifer?** easy to read.

Short chapters.

White space.

Pictures.

Big type for the big points.

Have it your way, as Burger King famously said.

And if you skipped this Introduction altogether, so be it.

Richard W. Lewis
April 2014

The course of what to do.

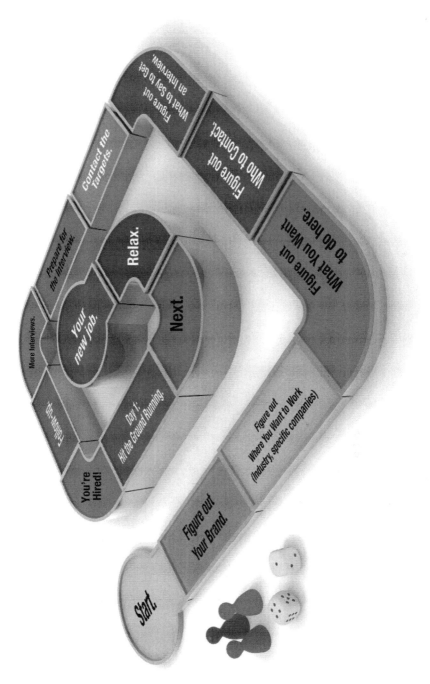

1

Why This Book Will Change Your Career-Hunting Life.

If it seems like it's more difficult than it used to be to get a good job, or really, any job, after graduating college, that's because, of course, it is.

When I graduated college 40 years ago I was one among one million grads. Today that number has climbed to nearly two million. Sure, the general population has grown as well but consider all the jobs in manufacturing that no longer exist and all the jobs that have gone global.

Some grads actually know what they're doing the day after graduation day besides sleeping very late. Many go on to professional school – medical, dental, law, and business – to fulfill their ambitions. Some enroll in graduate school, often postponing the day of reckoning. Medieval studies anyone?

And then there's what I call the Clarissa Syndrome. Clarissa is the tall blond; she went to Yale, speaks three languages, earned magna cum laude, was in a Secret Society (read: Network heaven), and sings Gilbert and Sullivan showtunes. All of them. In other words: Clarissa will get a job pretty much wherever she wants.

I wasn't a Clarissa back in 1974 and you probably aren't in 2014. But that doesn't mean you have to join Starbucks and be barista No. 49,365 either.

There is hope. You can learn how to brand and market yourself as I have taught scores of grads to do. Three reasons why I am qualified to write this book:

Unstoppable Clarissa.

One.

I spent a career in advertising, learning how to connect consumers to brands for some top companies around the world. I was in charge of the Absolut vodka advertising account for almost two decades, responsible for marketing, strategy and creative much of that time. It set the standard for creativity and innovation that other brands admired and copied.

Two.

I have taught the past six years, first at Yale and now at NYU a course I created called "Branding: People, Places & Things." This is an honors seminar that has helped expand my thinking by introducing me to college students who are on the road to figuring out their own Brands and need a guide. This book is an outgrowth of my course.

Three.

I have learned from my own three adult children (although they avoided virtually all my advice) and their friends, many who used me as the "guy who knows how to get people jobs." Not to mention I've learned from my wife, Isabel, who has been a recruiter for three decades.

When I started thinking about the job-career-life-hunting three years ago, something very obvious kept popping up. College students are often under-prepared by their campus career counselors. I had

assumed job-hunting advice in 2014 had to be better than it was for me. But then I started reading the cover letters and resumes of prospective job candidates. They didn't just all **look** the same, they **sounded** the same. I wondered if it were possible that everyone was told the best way to get a good job was to behave like everyone else.

It seems you have been told to dress like a sheep instead of dressing like yourself. You have been told to write the same cover letter as nearly everyone else. Why, I don't know. Except, perhaps, it's easy. But the result is everyone sounds dull from the get-go.

Which probably explains why there are professional resume-writing firms charging upwards of $1,000 to make you look interesting. (Or make you look like all the firm's other clients.) This is nothing short of a tragic expenditure.

I'm not interested in making you just look interesting. My goal is simply to present who you actually are, what differentiates you from your competition, enabling you to communicate what makes you unique. This is not magic. This is simply smart marketing.

What is smart marketing?

Let's use an example from the business world. Unless you're Samsung, which enjoys being the anti-Apple, you probably would be quite happy being Apple, currently the world's most valuable Brand.

They have a reputation for creating unique products and using design, technology, innovation and incredible attention to detail to command a top price wherever their products are sold.

Of course everyone can't be Apple. Sometimes even Apple doesn't behave like Apple. But even when Apple occasionally stumbles, it isn't for a lack of daring, soul-searching, and self-confidence.

Yet this wasn't always the case. Apple nearly didn't survive its adolescence in the 1990s. The products were over-priced, vanilla, and largely uninteresting. But even in its darkest days of flirting with bankruptcy, Apple never lost its attitude, its arrogance, even.

And neither should you.

2

The Heart
of the Matter.

When I started dabbling in helping recent grads, frustrated job-hunters, a lost soul here and there, to strike a path toward getting a decent job that might lead....to the next decent job, I launched "RL Career Services." No fancy-schmancy website, just a few pages of thoughts and a Craigslist ad. I offered, for $99 an hour of assessment, career guidance and a course of action. Money back guarantee, of course. After all, I had cut my teeth on straightening out dozens of my hires from my ad career, former students, my own kids' friends, and the occasional young man or woman on the street.

There was no shortage of early arrivals. Young adults, mostly 21-26, many already wearing the look of defeat, trying to get on track for a meaningful career, and with it, security, promise, and a decent apartment. Many suffered from the same symptoms:

- They graduated from a college that didn't have a Brand name that inspired oohs and ahs when they said it.

- They didn't have a 3.5+ GPA.

- They had already exhausted their limited, personal connections.

- They didn't have sparkling internships, leading in a straight line to a chosen career.

- They wanted to enter competitive fields:

advertising
fashion
public relations
social media
publishing
law
art
food
media

to name a few. (Strange: No one said, "I'm dying to get into life insurance.")

- They didn't feel special, didn't know how to really find a job, and didn't know what to do next, besides answer the ads on company job boards, Monster, Craigslist, Indeed, etc.

That's when I met Jennifer. (Of course that's not her real name, but she knows who she is.) Jennifer was starving to work in broadcasting. Literally. She worked part-time in a restaurant, lived full-time with her parents, and combed the ads for anything connected to radio or TV. She had graduated from a small college in Connecticut. B average. Sociology major. Pleasant personality. But I suspected there was more to Jennifer than she was telling me, so I scratched below the surface.

"Tell me more about yourself. What makes you smile? What do you do when you're not driving yourself crazy thinking about getting a job? Who are you?"

After poking around like this for a few minutes I found what I was looking for.

"Well, I'm a Scottish dancer."

More precisely, a competitive Scottish dancer! What's that? I sure didn't know.

Scottish dancing, or Scottish Highland dancing, has been around since the 19th Century, and is a big sport. It's a solo dance requiring great skill, technique, and stamina. One dances on the balls of the feet wearing special shoes called ghillies, a leather and lace operation.

Jennifer didn't think this was anything special, but I knew immediately it was. Plus she was good at it: She even had trophies. I had to convince her this was her ticket to the job she wanted.

"Richard, what does this have to do with TV?" she asked with more than a little wariness. *"It's simple, Jennifer: Scottish dancing is your special sauce. It demonstrates your uniqueness, drive, and passion. You'll see."*

We crafted a job campaign. She got two interviews within a week. And inside a month she got a job at a public TV station in Connecticut. But I got the bigger

payout. I figured out how to help people differentiate themselves from their competition. Plus, I got to learn about Scottish dancing.

How did Scottish dancing make Jennifer more hirable?

Finding a job, even a bad one, is a process. Finding a good job is typically a longer and tougher process. Candidates need to both differentiate themselves from other candidates on "paper," and they need to be outstanding in interviews. As I told Jennifer, her Scottish dancing demonstrated uniqueness, drive, and passion.

Uniqueness.

Of course she isn't the only Scottish dancer in the world but she's probably the only Scottish dancer the interviewer will ever meet. (And if by some coincidence the interviewer is also a Scottish dancer, there are bonus points for common experience.)

Drive.

Scottish dancing isn't learned overnight and isn't taught everywhere. To compete against the experts you have to, you guessed it, travel to Scotland. You have to work hard, select a goal, and figure out how to achieve it.

Passion.

Scottish dancing isn't just a resume builder; it has to be a passion. You have to really want to get good to get good. Focus. Practice. And probably a fair amount of solitary time unless you can trick your best friend into doing it, too.

Why do companies find this beneficial? Because you may very well have to demonstrate these qualities on the job, without the actual dancing. Or the interviewer may just want to learn what makes you tick. Or the interviewer would like to stay awake while interviewing you and this just sounds cool.

Character traits.

This may sound like a humanities course you managed to avoid in college but your character comes into play very early on in the screening process. Of course firms also prefer certain experience and skills, which you have or you don't. But if all else is even with other job candidates – on paper, before you've even met – you will have an edge when you demonstrate the character issues. And in some cases character issues will even overcome experience or skills deficits. Why? Because sometimes the humans in corporations act human, and may respond emotionally, that is, positively, toward a future Steve Jobs or Sheryl Sandberg.

What other character traits do companies seek?

Leadership.

Yes, you knew that already. Leadership is at the top of nearly everyone's list. Why? Because it's the sum of nearly all the other traits and, frankly, most people aren't leaders because it's difficult to be a leader. You may win a popularity contest to become the leader, but once there you'll surely lose the popularity contest if you're any good because you get to make the tough decisions that aren't popular. And if everyone were a leader, there wouldn't be any followers.

Examples: Perhaps you're a team captain, organization president, even a trip guide.

Teamwork.

Nearly every business has a collaborative aspect to its success. While top managers often create an environment of healthy competition among the lieutenants, more important is that people work well together, toward an agreed upon goal. (Although there's always at least one skunk in the works.)

Examples: member of an athletic team, orchestra or band.

Risk-Taking.

Ah, now I have your attention.

Risk-taking can be very tricky as a personal selling point. It can win or lose a meeting. Because risk-taking is often right on the fine line separating courage and foolishness. Which means it should be perceived as an acceptable risk taken to achieve a worthwhile goal.

Examples: Willing to be the first in nearly any endeavor.

Expertise.

This is a half-sister to uniqueness. You can be an expert in an endeavor that isn't unique. For instance, gems and rocks. Perhaps, you collected as a child, studied geology in school, and just became fascinated, so you read, explored, joined an organization, and eventually became something of an expert. Yet you decided while this was fun it wasn't what you wanted to do with your life. The qualities of becoming that expert – curiosity, analysis, and passion – may help find that great job.

I recognize this isn't an all-inclusive list. That is by design. I want to avoid, however, creating a Boy (or Girl) Scout manual where you feel the need to earn merit badges along every criteria. I want you to recognize there are components that will help make you successful in job-hunting as well as life-hunting, but this isn't a formula.

Think of it more as a recipe that permits and encourages experimentation. And while I have met many people, many types of people, perhaps I haven't met your type with your special recipe.

3

Finding the Scottish Dancer in You.

My underlying belief is everyone is unique, and it's often just a matter of finding the right bottle opener to release it, to reveal your uniqueness in order to establish your Brand.

Like most people, you probably don't think of yourself as the "Best" at something. As a result you may have stopped enjoying a certain activity such as playing the piano or playing baseball once you understood you would never be "good enough."

But your Brand isn't solely about achievement or fame. It's about the character traits that pushed you to pursue a certain activity in the first place: Passion, Risk-Taking, Teamwork, and so on.

You don't have to be the best to be good.

Here's an example from real life. My real life. My friend Jay graduated law school and, like all the other grads, prepped for the Bar Exam. It's the grueling, daylong test needed to practice law in every state. Jay studied for two months, took the prep course, and showed up for the test, ready, willing and able. He felt good about it. But the following month he learned he had failed it. Jay was disappointed but not crushed. He signed up again: Prepped longer, harder, even went to the gym to become more physically fit to take the exam. Boom! He failed again. Then, again. Even, again. All told, four swings, all misses. But on the fifth try: Success. Now if you speak to most lawyers they will tell you passing the Bar is a rite of passage and not a real determiner of how great a lawyer you will be. But Jay proved his desire, and dedication got him to his goal. It also demonstrates that hard work and stamina, seeing a task to the finish line, can overcome a natural inability to, say, pass an important test.

If I were reading this book, along about now I'd like a little help determining what MY special sauce is.

I don't dance particularly well, or so I've been told, let alone *Scottish* dance. Perhaps you could use a little cheat sheet to help locate some of the

- activities engaged
- experiences endured
- hurdles overcome

Chapter 3.

to help stand out from the competition.

That's why I've created this table to help find your sauce. These are just some examples of talents or experiences that you may overlook or simply underestimate. I encourage you to use it as a thought-starter to your own inventory, as opposed to reading the list searching for the box that fits you. Though, if the box fits, you're welcome to it.

What is **your** special sauce?

SKILL	PHYSICAL	MINDFUL	SELFLESS	OVERCOMIING ADVERSITY
Capoeira	Marathons	Organic Gardening	Tutoring	Deadbeat Dad
Milking Cows	Mountain Climbing	Monastic Retreat	Supporting your Family	Recovering from an Injury
Fencing	Swimming	Yoga	Started a Charity	Orphan
French Cooking	Krav Maga	Spelling Champ	Traveled to Help Victims of Nature	Overcoming a Stutter
Incense Making	Weight Lifting	Math Whiz	Volunteering at a Nursing Home	Emigrated from Another Country
Panning for Gold	Cycling	Coding		
Playing Viola	Archery			
Opera Singing				

Be aware of the talent turn-offs.

At some point in the future certain skills and activities may become valuable in securing a job but aren't yet seen in that light. Of course there are exceptions here so laugh as you might but realize most worthwhile opportunities will not ask how much time you spend each day on Facebook. Not to mention:

■ How successful you are at Fantasy Football.

■ How many Beer Pong tournaments you have won.

■ How many hours you spend on Call of Duty.

■ How many Starbucks you have visited.

■ How many tattoos you have.

■ How many countries you've visited.

I have actually seen these and worse offenders cited on candidate resumes without any sense of irony.

4

What is a Brand?
And Why Should
You Care?

You probably already know much about Brands. They have been in the marketing spotlight for at least 20 years but only in the past five years do they seem to have exploded, particularly as they relate to people.

Since I'm in the Branding sphere I naturally see mentions everywhere. And you probably have a sense of what they are but let me provide my version, too. I call my NYU course "Branding: People, Places & Things." Why? Because when I was in elementary school I learned that a proper noun, that is, one that began with a capital letter, is a person, place or thing. And while Brands weren't on most people's minds back in 1962 – including mine – it occurred to me that today, nearly all proper nouns aspire to become Brands.

That means not just cans of soup or cars or smartphones.

Brands are also countries, cities, and towns. You think about France differently than you think about China without necessarily having visited either. You have opinions about the people who live there, their food, their style and their attitude.

France is incredible Paris; liberté, egalité, fraternité; and of course, the Eiffel Tower. China is an evolving Brand of technology, growth, and an enormous population.

Will you ever again think about Malaysia without thinking about Malaysia flight #370?

People are also Brands. And not just the celebrated and famous, but really all of us who appear on Facebook and other social media, touting our tastes, our likes, the people and products we hug, and the all important pictures of ourselves looking happy, sad, busy, connected, and interesting.

I think of a Brand as the soup pot of qualities: Individual and identifiable ingredients, swimming and simmering, competing with our other ingredients to be noticed, loved, and rewarded.

A particular Brand is the sum total of all the attitudes and opinions living in our minds about a Person,

Chapter 4

Place or Thing.

Let's consider the world's most famous Brand, Coca Cola, and all the dimensions and traits that come to mind about Coca Cola. We discover how much we know about Coke from what they tell us and show us. We also learn about Coke from what others tell us. And we fill in the blanks from our own experience.

Just think of the word "Brand" as another word for "reputation." Coke **created** its reputation with but a single product. Fast forward one hundred years to a universe of products, flavors, packages, ads, and messages.

Until recently there was a two-direction flow of chatter: From the Brand and Toward the Brand.

But with the Internet and the advent of social media there's now a third direction: Consumers and non-consumers alike, now **control** the reputation because we can talk, photo, and write each other INSTANTLY.

Name.	Coca Cola, Coke, Diet Coke, etc.
Product.	Brown sugar water.
Package.	The short, green, glass bottle, the original Coke icon, whose image even appears on the cans.
Color.	Red.
Taste.	Sweet. Even when it's low calorie or zero calorie.
Smell.	Bubbly and sweet. Yes, you can inhale the bubbles.
Sound.	The gas release *Psshhh* you hear upon opening.
Available.	Everywhere.
Words.	Refresh. Happiness. Pop. Classic.

Other symbols.	Santa. Polar Bears.
Social.	"Things go better with Coke." "Open Happiness."
Archenemy.	Pepsi.
Typeface.	Old-fashioned script

New-fashioned bold.

Coke

Customers.	Everyone.

Even within this inventory of easy to compile attributes is the understanding that the Coca Cola Company is big and rich and famous, yet it isn't entirely responsible for its Brand. In fact, you are. Because there are qualities that people describe to the Brand that Coke isn't saying such as:

Unhealthy.   Empty, sugary calories leading to obesity, tooth decay and diabetes.

Habit-forming.   Not like tobacco, of course, but just watch a child drink one. Caffeine and sugar are powerful habit makers.

We talk to each other about the Brand......

We talk to each other about the Brand...

You

We talk to each other about the Brand...

We talk to each other about the Brand......

You

We talk to each other

We talk to each oth...

You

You talk to the Brand......

The Brand talks to you ......

Back to you.

When it comes down to it, you aren't all that different from Coke. You create an image, a persona, a Brand that you present to the world. The world – or some of it – inhales, chews, massages, and spits back their version of you. Some of it you created, some of which is created for you.

Early on in my course I teach my students a simple definition of a Brand. It appears early on the Marty Neumeier's book, **The Brand Gap**.

Neumeier says a Brand is a person's gut *feeling* (italics mine) about a product, service or company. I like gut feeling. While the actual gut is more likely in your stomach, in this case the gut feels like a mash-up of the head and the heart, the result of all the arithmetic in our heads as to how we feel about something. It's our uncensored opinion. It's honest.

It isn't necessarily what we would say to the Brand if its representatives were in the room with us. (Perhaps we don't want to hurt their feelings.)

It's more like what we say when the Brand isn't in the room. It's out of earshot. We don't care if we hurt its feelings. Understanding this will help you come to terms with your Brand, what your audiences say when you're not in the room about your reputation.

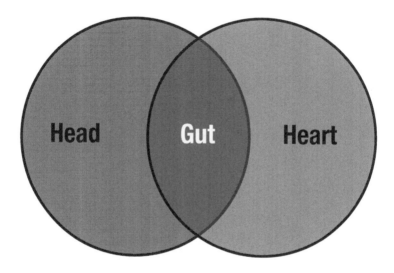

5

Brand You.

The concept of a personal Brand is a recent phenomenon. Some attribute it to the 1981 Trout & Ries classic marketing text, **Positioning: The Battle for Your Mind.** Business guru, Tom Peters, is credited for popularizing it in 1997. My sense is it exploded in the mid-2000s as celebrities increasingly cashed in on their names to market books, videos, food, beverages, perfumes, diets, and virtually any business they could lend their name to.

No doubt, the rise of social media has encouraged, if not required, people to express their personal Brand via Facebook, Instagram, Tumblr, and the like. We are the sum of our friends and family, music and movies, sunrises and sunsets, not to mention that last great cup of coffee consumed at Newark Airport. (Now, that's an oxymoron.)

What was once thought of as a tool for self-help has evolved into a tool for self-promotion. We shout, *"Look at me: Don't you just love me?"*

Because some celebrity Brands dip in to the Bay of Excess (not a real place) it can ruin it for the rest of us.

The media will hammer them even while we, the consumers, can't get our fill.

Just think of the Kardashian empire. Donald Trump. Martha Stewart. Miley Cyrus. You're thinking, I wouldn't mind their branding problems if they come with their branding riches.

Typically, a well-known person becomes a Brand when she transforms the equity of her name from one realm to another. For instance, a comedian on *Saturday Night Live* becomes an actor and a United States Senator. Think Al Franken. Or a recording artist becomes an actor, becomes a Silicon Valley honcho. Think Justin Timberlake. Or a singer becomes an actress, becomes a poster child for drug- alcohol- and auto-abuse. Think Lindsay Lohan.

Personal branding for the rest of us.

There are a lot of the rest of us, too.

7,000,000,000,000

Seven billion people
on the planet.

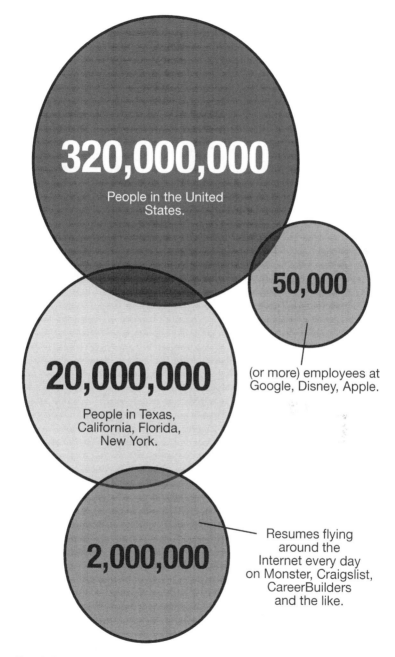

320,000,000

People in the United States.

50,000

(or more) employees at Google, Disney, Apple.

20,000,000

People in Texas, California, Florida, New York.

2,000,000

Resumes flying around the Internet every day on Monster, Craigslist, CareerBuilders and the like.

These balloons are not to scale, but just for illustrative purposes.

You get the point. You don't need me to shrink your ego. I am going to help you create, refine, and project your Brand. Once you have a smarter way to think about yourself in the marketplace, you can launch and grow your career in a way that 80% of your competition doesn't know how to do. Correction: Make that 90%.

I have analyzed the leading personal Brand components toward understanding what makes people successful. More precisely, the components people believe will make them successful.

You may ask, what is success? While we all may define it differently, I bet nearly everyone would agree with this:

Success Is The Accomplishment Of One's Goals.

At least, that's my definition.

But what's important here is that YOU take control of the definition of success. That YOU own it. Success should be seen through your eyes, not those of your parents, friends, or people laying in wait to judge you.

6

The Sexy Six.

The sexy six components leading to success.
(And, no, sexy isn't on the list.)

Appearance.
Brains.
Connections.
Drive.
Personality.
Talent.

Appearance.

While the most beautiful and handsome among us rarely acknowledge beauty to be a factor in their success, I don't know any beautiful people who would be willing to trade their looks. We revere beauty. We vote for the more handsome presidential candidates. Think Obama vs. McCain, Clinton vs. George H. Bush, Reagan vs. Carter. *New York Times* writer Andrew Ross Sorkin calls it the "CEO Beauty Premium." Citing a University of Wisconsin study that found "a CEO's appearance had a positive and significant impact on stock returns surrounding the first day the CEO is on the job." And "a one-point increase in attractiveness on a ten-point scale is related to a huge increase in total wage." Tall people make more money than short people. An attractive set of teeth can be the difference of getting or not getting a job.

Message: **Everyone has at least a slice of beauty. Make the absolute most of your appearance. It can simply be a winning smile or a twinkle in the eye. While you can't undo Mother Nature, don't undermine her by dressing slovenly or putting too much emphasis on solutions from a bottle.**

Brains.

When I say brains, I'm thinking of an obvious and powerful intelligence. It doesn't have to be genius-level à la Stephen Hawking, but that sure wouldn't hurt. It can be a smart intelligence; think how people often compare book smarts to street smarts, usually smearing the former if they have the latter. Think of the ability to analyze, to solve problems. Think chess: The ability to look-ahead and predict based on likely possibilities and probabilities. People who can do that have brainpower.

Message: The next best thing to brains is knowledge. We gain knowledge through life experience and, especially, reading. Nearly one-third of Americans don't read a single book in a year. Don't be that person. Pick a subject, an author, an anything, and read all about it.

Connections.

Ah, connections. Just saying it makes me, uh, jealous, of people with connections. I think this is the number one envied component of success. They cry, "It's not what you know, but who you know." The image of the silver spoon in the infant's mouth, the golden last name of Kennedy, Clinton and Hilton. The name, alone, opens locked doors; at least we want to believe. But remember, there are certain expectations placed upon the individual who walks through the door: You still have to perform, sometimes even better than the person without the connection.

Message: **It's said that strangers are just people you haven't yet met. Everyone you meet may become the person who opens your significant door. Later, when successful, you will become the person others see as their connection.**

Drive.

People with drive, real drive, just don't give up when everyone else would. (Winston Churchill: "Never give up, never, never.") Drive is the component that overcomes extreme obstacles: Disability, crappy childhood, no money, or competition for resources. Drive is ambition's smart brother. And it's something of a lost quality in America, unless you just immigrated and know, firsthand, how tough things can be.

Chapter 6

Message: *I've always appreciated people who tell me I can't do something. It gives me the drive to prove them wrong. And I still remember the mantra I learned in kindergarten: "If at first you don't succeed, try, try, again."*

Personality.

A winning personality is a set of qualities (as opposed to a single one) that makes an individual likable, thus encouraging others to hang around with you. These qualities are typically un-measurable (by scale or ruler) yet also immeasurable (limitless). We say someone may be fun to be around, is high-energy, good-humored, empathetic or interesting. We try to avoid negative people – and well we should – because negativity is both a downer and contagious.

Message: *Whenever I need to be reminded of the power of personality, I listen to the Lloyd Price recording of the song called "Personality." He sings: "Because you've got personality, walk, talk, style, charm, plus you've got a great big heart." I think it's the great big heart that's the key to all the other stuff.*

Talent.

We often hear of "God-given" talents such as hitting a baseball, acting on stage, or painting a portrait. We admire, respect, and are often in awe of extreme talent. Yes, we all have the seed of talent – a natural ability – to do something remarkably well, no doubt, but talent isn't destiny. It has to be identified, nourished, chaperoned, and cultivated. And when that happens, people take notice. We admire talent because it is so visible, and sometimes even unique. We observe, "He has a talent for making money," making it sound like an extension of his natural senses. We may even say he has a nose for it.

Message: **Jennifer wasn't born a Scottish dancer. She became one.**

Many people excel at more than one of these qualities. Isn't that intimidating! It may seem unfair that somebody is beautiful, talented and connected while so many people are seemingly, in baseball parlance, 0 for 6.

You are now perhaps thinking, "Ugh, I'm cooked.

I'm not special along any of these dimensions."
Of course, you're not cooked. But to continue the metaphor, you are in the oven. You do have to determine what you have to identify as your not-so-secret weapon, as well as how to increase its value and communicate it to your target audiences.

7

Getting Started on Brand You.

Create a personal inventory.

This isn't anywhere near as overwhelming as it sounds. Think of your personal inventory as your mind's storage room: The stuff that makes you, you. It's the collection of your life's experiences, learning, talents, attitudes and assets, which you will employ to shape your future.

Getting started is easier than it sounds. Find a quiet place. Open a new Word document or scribble on a blank page of a yellow pad. Use these categories as thought starters. Or create your own. Then begin writing down thoughts of:

Activities you enjoy. Dismantle Car Engines. Speaking Arabic. Meditating.

Accomplishments: Athletic, Artistic, Education, Social, Community, Business.

Aspirations: Space Travel. App Creator. First Woman President.

Crazy Stuff. Peanut Butter Connoisseur. Bird Watcher. Dinosaur Bone Hunter.

Family: Are you the Genius, Peacemaker, or

Troublemaker?

Amazing physical feats. Climbed a Volcano. Swam a Three-Mile Lake.

The point is, write everything down. Don't edit as you go along. (Because when you do that, you're neither writing nor editing.)

This should fill a couple of pages. Now, go back and circle the items that most fit, that set you apart from the rest of us. This exercise will be the foundation of your personal Brand. Perhaps you decide your most evident personal characteristic is your winning attitude. You have that (Winston) Churchillian gene, which means you never give up, despite the odds or the score.

Now it's time to focus on the more interesting pieces of you. It may not be a single attribute as much as a collection or handful that draw your picture.

1. You enjoy solving puzzles: Crosswords, brainteasers; you read mysteries because you like following the clues and predict the secret killer at the end. You think, this sounds pretty mundane. But together they reveal you're very analytical and probably don't quit until you find the solution. Even when you take a break, you're still thinking about it in the "back" of your brain.

2. You're on your college fencing team. You're very good, even competed in tourneys around the country as a teenager. But you have come to hate fencing: it takes up too much time, you get anxious before each match, and you'd rather be doing twenty other activities. But you don't quit. Why? Because you're on a team, and you don't want to let your teammates down, you don't want the coach to hate you, and you want to act like an adult with responsibilities, even if this is an "elective" activity.

Look at all the qualities you've demonstrated for an activity you no longer even like: Teamwork, respect, "stick-to-it-ness" in an era when people can't even commit to making a phone call.

3. You bake pies. And have been doing it since your Mom taught you. First, you only baked one pie, peach, until it was perfect. You did it over and over again. You changed the recipe a dozen times and became confident that your instincts, your creativity unleashed through experience, opened up new pie vistas. Then you began selling pies to friends and neighbors. You even opened up a pie stand on your country road. You learned how to deal with customers, even the mean ones. You interested a restaurant into carrying your pies on its menu. You are a self-taught marketing person!

Chapter 7.

Test your Brand.

Approach a family member or close friend, someone who knows you well and is comfortable talking to you about you. Find out if what you think about yourself sounds true to him. You don't have to ask if your winning attitude sounds like a good Brand. That isn't their assignment unless they are also reading this book. You want them to respond to your self-awareness, not your marketing skills. Does what you have written down sound like a legitimate you?

Remember, you are already a unique person.
There isn't yet a clone or android version of you in the marketplace. But the competition can be pretty severe.

You understand only one person can be the absolute best at any endeavor. But striving for number one in practically any activity is both self-improving and acknowledged by others as worthy and respected.

Consider: One of the most famous – and successful – advertising campaigns of the 20th Century was for Avis Rent-A-Car. As the perennial also-ran to industry leader, Hertz, they made a virtue of their runner up status by declaring: ***"Because we are only No. 2 – We try harder."*** Ah, effort. It opened the door to every runner-up in every business to pitch themselves as the underdogs. And since there is but one No.1, aren't we all underdogs?

Your First Job isn't Your Last Job.

First-time job hunters, particularly before or after graduating college, often make a colossal mistake.

(I first crossed out "colossal," thought about it, and then retyped it because I really mean it.)

What is that mistake?

They give up.

First, of course, they decide to pursue a particular area or industry, often a seemingly more glamorous one like TV, music, advertising, fashion and so on. Grads quickly exhaust their personal contacts, apply to some company job-sites, and may even use some of the methods I will discuss in future chapters. But all to no avail. So what do they do?

They essentially get back into bed, pull the covers over their heads, and take a self-pity nap.

They cry, *"There are no suitable jobs out there! How unfair! I'm a college grad! Why doesn't anyone want me?"*

Plus, they may be sitting on tens of thousands of dollars of debt, money that enabled them to go to college. They may also be under the harsh light of their parents' scrutiny and the *"Who told you to major in Renaissance painters in the first place?"*

The problem, however, is not with the job market – which is always difficult to crack for certain fields – but with the grads' attitude.

These grads are wearing the tight-fitting, inflexible coat called, *"I will only go to work where I want to work!"*

Sound like anyone you know?

Understand: there is a third option between doing nothing, and I mean nothing, and working at Starbucks or the local fitness center.

That option is working at non-glamorous businesses in order to

- Get some legitimate post-college work experience
- Make some money to pay living expenses
- Not squander your 20s: some of the best years of your life

Every fall I meet grads who look like they've been hit in the head with a punch from "the real world," telling them they aren't "good enough," but what they really need is a smack in the head to pursue a slightly different path.

For instance, say you're interested in marketing and want to join an advertising or media firm but the jobs are scarce and crazy-competitive.

Guess what? Marketing and all its tools are now essential departments in a variety of firms: law, accounting, medical, and nearly all non-profits. Every business needs to differentiate itself, discover its Brand, and attract more customers. Who knew? Not everyone. But now you do.

Which means you need to set your sights, first, on what you **want** to be doing, more than **where** you want to be doing it.

You will gain valuable experience, demonstrating, and don't laugh, that you can get a job and keep a job! All the while you will make money, make contacts, and, dare I say, feel better about yourself.

I know what some of you are still thinking: Good grief, Lewis wants me to go work at an insurance firm. He's got to be kidding! What will my friends say?

They'll say you're smart enough to get off your ass. And while you're climbing that Wall of Worry, you might also ask: *"But won't I get stuck in that business and never get out?"*

Not at all. You'll develop skills, earn experience, and make yourself more marketable when you're ready to look for your second job and third job.

This is not 1960, when workers expected, even sought, one company and one career for the next 40 years. *The Wall Street Journal* predicts people entering the work force today will have seven different careers before they retire.

Do you need any more reasons to stop doing nothing and start doing something?

9

How and Why to Reach Out to Prospective Companies.

Let's consider all the possible ways you could get an interview at a firm where you want to work. Then, let's change the way you approach the task, using a method 90% of your job-seeking competitors don't.

Campus interviews. If you're still a student, obviously, it's great to get on-campus interviews. They offer real companies hiring for real jobs. While many desirable firms have cut back their interviewing, some actually just interview for window-dressing. (Good PR, maintaining goodwill at certain campuses where they have a history and want to maintain good relations until times improve.) You likely know it's very difficult to get the coveted interview slots. And since recruiters interview at multiple campuses, the odds are not in your favor.

Personal connections. Of course these are great to have, but usually become exhausted quickly because even the very top executives are besieged.
Tom Carroll, the CEO of advertising agency TBWA Worldwide, receives over 500 personal referrals just for the agency's New York summer intern program which may hire only ten interns. Your uncle Fred

wants to help, as does your neighbor Roxanne. By all means, seek it out, but understand the connections tap out soon.

Company job boards. Some firms display available jobs right on their websites. Aggregator sites then repost them on their sites. Often the jobs are long gone by the time you see a post, because it's simply not a priority of firms to take down the listing. They may simply want to create a resume bank for the future, or they haven't gotten around to physically removing the listing. Either way, you are probably one among hundreds – if not thousands – applying for a desirable job.

Monster, Career Builder, Craigslist, etc. Simply, they are a necessary evil. You have to check them out, but, like company job boards, they are like the New Orleans Super Dome after Hurricane Katrina: People go there because there's no place better to go, even though there are holes in the ceiling letting in the rain. All right, maybe there aren't holes in the ceiling. But these sites are a bizarre bazaar and not the first place or last place to go when you're job hunting.

Chapter 9

Job candidates go there because it's easy and it feels productive, even if it isn't. But consider: these sites receive thousands of resumes the first few days, hundreds in the first few minutes.

Headhunters. Also known as recruiters and personnel agencies, they sometimes have good jobs for college graduates because they have relationships with client companies who trust the headhunters to send only their best people. They are typically very busy and focus on filling the positions they have; they aren't employment counselors or social workers. Treat them with respect and do not waste their time.

Company HR Departments. You figure, HR (or Human Resources), is the place to send a resume. If so, you're probably wrong. While many firms have HR departments staffed with sympathetic humans, you have to remember their loyalties are always with their employers, and not with the job candidates. Applicants are often confused, thinking the H in HR stands for them. It doesn't. The H should actually be a "C" because the C stands for Corporate, and their jobs are to protect the company and its management.

These people can also be notoriously two-faced once you meet. They may even hug you! Don't let them do that. They are like polar bears: gentle-looking but they will eat you in an instant. More importantly for the job-hunter, HR is like the U.S. Post Office "dead letter" file: Resumes come in like letters to Santa but, unlike Santa, they aren't read, replied, or even filed. The most junior person in the department may be assigned to review them, but that's actually pretty rare. The major exception is when resumes are "sent down" from company executives, because then they are practically personal referrals from people already in the firm.

Up to now I've painted a bleak picture of tactics everyone uses but only work for the few. Now I will tell you how to do it differently.

Ah, company executives: Directors, Managers, Presidents!

These are the folks you want to contact. Presidents, Department Heads, senior people, specific individuals in the departments where you want to work. Why?

Because these people are the engines of the company. They create the product or ideas or stuff the company makes or sells. They make things happen. They bring in the money. Their work pays the bills.

Many are always looking for new blood, perhaps not at the precise moment you contact them but when you arrive, packaged, as the exciting version of yourself – your Brand – one of three things will happen.

Beware the HR bears.

1. They will meet you.
2. They will pass you on to someone else to meet you, maybe even HR, but with their imprimatur. (That means: I like this guy so see him!)
3. They will do nothing.

But look: two out of three possibilities are good for you. That's better odds than a pass thrown by a NFL quarterback where two out of three possibilities – an incompletion or interception – are bad for the team.

It can take a little detective work to find them.

The first place to look is on the company websites. Some include all significant employees and their contact info. Some sites just include officers. You can phone and ask, "Who is responsible for?" If you get a live person they may even be allowed to answer the question. Some firms do, some don't.

Next, you want to check LinkedIn. You have to sign up – it's free – and post your profile. LinkedIn has a lot of powerful search tools to find company employees by industry, company name, and individual's name. It will also reveal who you know who may already know personnel you want to meet.

There are pay services such as Hoover's and The List, to name two, which are online directories of firms and their employees. But for *no* money you can just Google people, using search terms "President of…" or "Person who runs…" It's your Internet, use it.

You may be wondering.

Why might the President like you when HR ignores you? The exec admires your smarts for finding him; your moxie, for contacting him; and he probably likes what you've written because you have custom-tailored the letter to him. That's right, a good old-fashioned letter.

10

The Cover Letter is not the Chaperone to the Resume.

The cover letter has the dumbest name going.
It practically shouts,

*"This doesn't count, don't spend any time reading it,
go right to my resume"*

Which explains why 90% of applicants do a crappy,
yes, crappy, job on it. However, the truth couldn't be
more opposite than the conventional knowledge.

It's really simple to understand:

Every contact with a target firm is an opportunity to
sell you, to get you to the next stage of hiring.
If all your cover letter says is, in effect, *"Here comes
my resume!!"* how exciting is that?

And when you realize your resume has to follow a
certain rigid format and maintain a high level of
seriousness, your cover letter should be more like
Ryan Seacrest introducing American Idol contestants
and sound less like the mailman introducing the
accountant.

So, forget everything you ever knew about cover letters. If you don't know anything, it's even better. When you write a great cover letter or email, the reader will want to meet you even without reading the resume. It's an opportunity to use your creativity to sell yourself, which you can't do in a resume. It's also an opportunity to demonstrate at least a thimbleful of knowledge about the position or company that you're applying to. Finally, it's the chance to suggest a "next step" beyond the inert line: "I look forward to hearing from you."

Let's look at those four easy steps:

1. This is an opening sentence and support that declares what your Brand or specialness or secret sauce is.

2. These are the two or three sentences that demonstrate your understanding of the person/job/company you're writing about.

3. These are the two or three sentences explaining why you would fit in at that organization.

4. This is the pro-active next step to distinguish yourself from the passive turtles that cross their little paws waiting to hear if they are good enough to be contacted for an interview.

Here are a few real-life examples:

Jennifer Cotten

Dear Mr. Davenport,

When I was twelve I took up Scottish dancing. While I have no Scottish "blood," I became interested because it required intense focus to learn all the proper moves, the competition offered me a chance to travel, and I could excel at something both fun and very challenging.

As a media executive at WMOX, I'm sure you feel similarly: Broadcasting culture news to a television audience that is always looking for the "new" is 90% challenging and 10% fun.

As a Media Studies grad from Boston University I have more than an inkling what it takes to begin a career at WMOX. And as someone who just won the Edinburgh Prize for Young Adults, I can appreciate the drive it takes to be successful.

I'll contact you later in the week to see if you would be available to talk about future opportunities at WMOX.

Sincerely,

Jennifer Cotten

Jennifer Cotten

1. Notice the first sentence provides Jennifer's uniqueness – Scottish Dancing – and her early commitment. Then she provided the personal qualities without hammering them.

2. She took a leap that Davenport's job is a little similar to Scottish Dancing: fun and challenging. Perhaps she read something about him; perhaps she just made it up.

3. Jennifer then describes her educational preparation with a current achievement as an adult.

4. She closes the note with the promise to take the initiative and contact him later in the week. Of course this doesn't rule out Davenport contacting her first.

Dan Glass

Dear Mr. Adams,

I eat challenges for breakfast.

Seven years ago I injured my pitching arm during a routine practice. It required surgery and a lengthy rehab. I learned that hard work, optimism, and a great team helped me overcome.

I face a similar challenge today: Finding a career-building position utilizing my Master's in Accounting, banking experience, and positive attitude.

While it's presumptuous to assume Chase has a current opening matching my skills and attitude, I would welcome the chance to discuss a future opportunity.

I'll contact you later in the week to schedule time for a conversation.

Best,

Dan Glass

Dan Glass

1. Opening paragraphs can take a different approach. Here is a strong, memorable first sentence followed by a life-building experience creating the attitude.

2. "Unreasonable to assume company has a current opening" demonstrates an understanding there aren't jobs waiting for you the moment you contact a firm.

3. Dan asks for a conversation: a short, no-promises commitment from Mr. Adams.

Dear Mr. Terry,

My Japanese-born Mom reluctantly named me Gary. Twenty years later, imagine my discomfort living in Tokyo, introducing myself to countless giggles, finally to learn that "Gary" is Japanese for "diarrhea."

I understand Cranium Architects is developing its marketing department and broadening its East Asian presence. Your recent AIA commendation speaks to writing's increased criticality in your practice.

At the AIA I completed a writing-intensive Master's in the history of architecture where writing and an ease of presentation were critical to my success. At NYU, studies of Japanese architecture led to a fellowship in Japan – and, well, that unfortunate realization.

Perhaps, you may have time for a coffee to talk about future prospects in your marketing department. I'll contact you later in the week.

Best,

Gary Wolf

1. Gary's opening anecdote speaks to his humility and is just the right length.

2. He uses knowledge gleaned on the Web to demonstrate he is following the firm.

3. Gary then describes his qualifications for consideration.

4. He ends on a suggestion for coffee, a small commitment of time.

Dear Ms. Florentine,

Mark Zuckerberg has nothing on me.
Except, perhaps, a few billion dollars.

Perhaps, in twenty years, social media will be a relic. But, today, it's the two-way circulatory system between a business and all its audiences: customers, friends, and the media.

Having spent the last two years creating and implementing the official Facebook site at my school, Occidental College, I understand how vital a communications tool it is, where timely and reliable information is paramount.

Given how critical communications is at Avon with its multiple audiences, perhaps we could meet to discuss some ideas I'd like to share to help upgrade your already outstanding efforts.

I'll call you on Friday to arrange a mutually convenient time.

Best,

Phoebe Bauer

Phoebe Bauer

1. Phoebe exudes confidence and light-heartedness from the start.

2. She demonstrates a long view of her current skill, providing specific experience

3. She both compliments the firm and commits to share her ideas to help them.
(Now she just has to come up with a few ideas, probably the easy part.)

What do all these "cover letters" have in common?

They have personality.

Your personality. Your specialness. Your Brand.

They are customized to that firm.

Which means the reader believes it didn't come from a cover letter factory.

They demonstrate what you can do and what you're looking for.

Because you have thought about it and written it clearly.

They include a next step: Yours.

This demonstrates you know how to follow-up even if you don't have to. Plus there's a very good chance you will hear from the person before you contact him again.

They don't demand a lot of time.

A conversation. A coffee.

They recognize there very likely isn't a job open at the moment you write the letter.

Which means you're planting for the future.

And many times there are jobs that haven't been announced yet and you put yourself on the early track.

They don't even mention your resume is attached.

Go ahead. Attach the resume. They'll see it's there, even without the "more interesting stuff about me is attached" line.

Short is sweet.

Mark Twain famously wrote, and I famously remember:

"Sorry I didn't have time to write a short letter; so I wrote a long one instead."

11

More Than a Few Words About Resumes.

There are hundreds, if not thousands, of books written about how to write a winning resume. This book isn't one of them. If that is what you think you need just take a quick scan at Amazon. These are just the books on the first page with "Dead" in the title!

The Resume is Dead
Resumes are Dead
Knock 'Em Dead Resumes

People talk about resumes as though they are biblical: precious documents that are a matter of life and death, the difference between success and failure, wealth and poverty. They may also warn if you don't prepare and design your resume "their" way, you may as well become a monk and join a monastery. (Though I hear even monasteries require resumes for admission.)

If you've never written a resume then you need some guidance. But don't be tricked into believing there is a right way and a wrong way.

Resumes are a little like haircuts: Some people look good only one way; others look great with any hairstyle they choose.

Just as we want to believe that if we dye our hair blonde, we will become more fun, attractive and sexy, we want to believe that if we discover the right combination of resume elements and lay them out perfectly for all to see, then we will get that great job.

We want to believe that it's the resume that is the passkey to our futures, so we place a huge emotional investment in them. I'm convinced the reason we fear its failure to impress is because it represents our personal failure. As soon as we engrave our life on two pages of black-and-white text, it can feel so thin, so inadequate. It's a mirror of our feelings of inadequacy.

In truth, it doesn't even get better as we secure jobs, acquire experience, and develop expertise. As a marketing exec I was tinkering with my resume into my 50s, trying to keep it (me) relevant and posting a narrative of my business life as though it proceeded in a straight line, one designed by me thirty years prior. What a bucket of pig slop that is! It just never ends. Recruiters and HR departments are addicted to resumes and their black and white version of our lives. They become nervous when we diverge from a rigid resume style of dates, titles, duties, and accomplishments. Just as they would if we were to arrive for an interview not wearing any shoes. Some think: This person cannot draw within the frame and will not fit in here.

A few years ago I chose a different resume path. But then I could afford to because, self-employed, I was no longer seeking a job-job. And while I received many compliments for its "different-ness" I know it also made some people uneasy. I include it here because I think my "resume" is still relevant for me and it may give you an idea of what can be done if you chuck the rules.

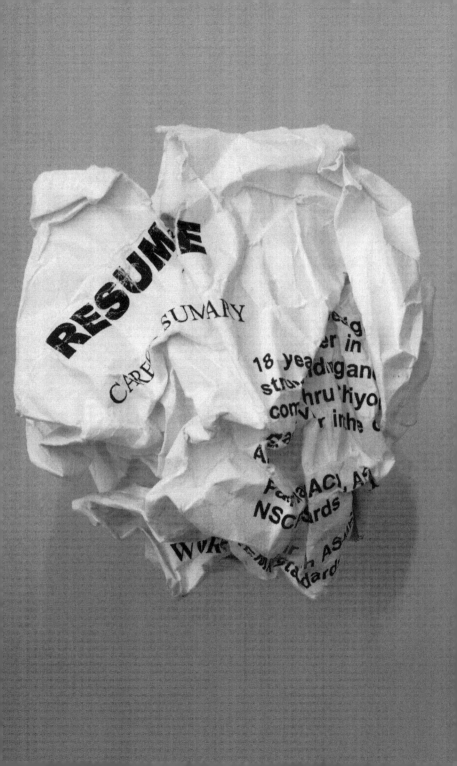

RICHARD LEWIS-ISMS

Coining Phrases since 1962...
"Life is a frequency medium."
"You can never have too many napkins in this life."
"The next best thing to a 'yes' is a fast 'no'."
"If you tell the truth nine straight times, you can have fun on the tenth."
"Free food tastes better."
"Things could be worse but should be better."
(Richard Lewis, second from right)

Richard Lewis, Marketing Doctor

RICHARD WAS THE WORLDWIDE ACCOUNT DIRECTOR FOR **ABSOLUT** AT TBWA/CHIAT/DAY.

HE WAS RESPONSIBLE FOR MARKETING, STRATEGY AND CREATIVE.

THERE, HE CREATED AND COLLABORATED ON MANY OF THE CAMPAIGN'S MOST LOVED ADS.

PROFILE

Advertising and marketing executive, best-selling author, strategist, idea person, speaker, and professor. Dynamic team leader and motivator, possessing a business head and a creative heart.

RICHARD LEWIS

RL IDEAS, LTD
BRANDING
STRATEGY
INNOVATION

914.527.7574
RL@rlconsulting.biz

Dedicated on June 8, 2004, following 17 years of service to ABSOLUT.
Permanent installation:
19A Arstaangsvagen, Stockholm, Sweden.

ABSOLUT BOOK.

ABSOLUT SEQUEL.

NEW YORK TIMES BEST-SELLING AUTHOR

425,000 copies sold. Named "must have" marketing books by Stuart Elliott, *New York Times*; *Advertising Age*, *Adweek*.

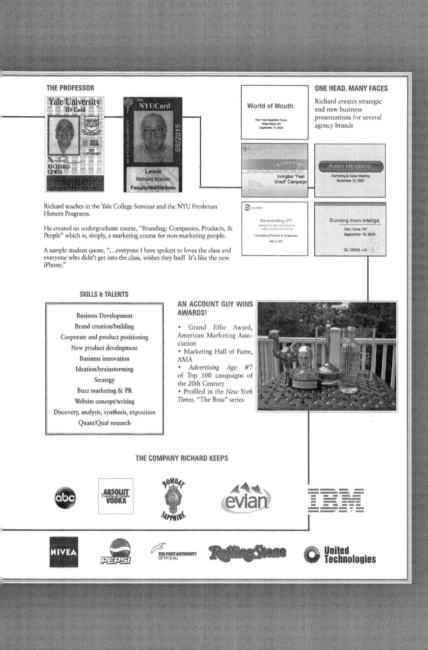

THE PROFESSOR

Richard teaches in the Yale College Seminar and the NYU Freshman Honors Programs.

He created an undergraduate course, "Branding: Companies, Products, & People" which is, simply, a marketing course for non-marketing people.

A sample student quote, "...everyone I have spoken to loves the class and everyone who didn't get into the class, wishes they had! It's like the new iPhone."

ONE HEAD, MANY FACES

Richard creates strategic and new business presentations for several agency brands

SKILLS & TALENTS

Business Development
Brand creation/building
Corporate and product positioning
New product development
Business innovation
Ideation/brainstorming
Strategy
Buzz marketing & PR
Website concept/writing
Discovery, analysis, synthesis, exposition
Quant/Qual research

AN ACCOUNT GUY WINS AWARDS!

• Grand Effie Award, American Marketing Association
• Marketing Hall of Fame, AMA
• *Advertising Age* #7 of Top 100 campaigns of the 20th Century
• Profiled in the *New York Times*, "The Boss" series

THE COMPANY RICHARD KEEPS

Now that I hope I have made you less intimidated by the resume devil, here are some guidelines before you even put fingers to keyboard.

The resume is a representation of you. You are not a representation of it.

Be sure you understand your specialness, positioning, and Brand before you write your resume. Because you want to be sure to find the way to include it from the beginning; as journalists say, "Don't bury the lead" and make the reader discover it on the last line of, say, "Personal Interests."

Don't write anything that can be disproved.

That's a polite way of saying don't tell any factual lies: Dates, places, titles, deeds or anything else I didn't include. The penultimate thing that can happen is you will not pass a reference check before being offered a job. The ultimate thing that can happen is you can actually get fired from a job you start if the reference check continued beyond your start date. This is not moral advice; this is a commandment.

Chapter 11

Do not pay someone $1,000 to write your resume.

Personally, I believe everyone should write his or her own resumes, but I understand that isn't always the best option. Often you can work with a parent, friend, or coach to help unfurl your story in a creative and cohesive manner. Sometimes this may even cost some money. But you're not the SVP/Marketing at Pepsi, so you don't need to spend $1,000, $1,500, or even $2,500, because that's what some resume services charge. I have met with a couple of these services, not for the purpose of doctoring my resume but to help them market their services, and I understand they are tweaking people's egos as much as their resumes.

Feel comfortable writing a job or career objective.

Hey, it demonstrates you know what you're looking for, even if when you get there you discover you're looking for something else. It's the first thing people will read, so demonstrate the sum of your self-understanding to the firm receiving it. Plus, it's an easy section to revise if you apply to very diverse firms or positions.

One page? Two pages? Etc.

Length isn't as long as it once was, as most resumes are read on screen. But there is something elegant in painting your life so far on a single canvas. So if there is a page two, you better have some meat and potatoes on it, stuff that is worth knowing about you.

Perfection in the little things.

One of companies' favorite ways to give you no thought whatsoever is to discover typos or other tiny errors that says to them: You didn't proofread the most important document of your life! Don't give them that out. The best method: Print it and show it to "new eyes," and challenge those eyes to find a mistake.

Don't be afraid of looking good.

There once was a time where firms frowned on professional-looking resumes. That even sounds funny as I write it. It meant people who went to printing or design companies for resume preparation. But that was before all the tools you now have on hand: Word, PhotoShop, Illustrator, etc. And if you're contacting a creative business in the arts, marketing, fashion, to name just a few, you have a lot more leeway and freeway to demonstrate skills and originality.

Make the robots happy.

Many firms use ATS programs. These are Applicant Tracking Systems that seek certain keywords in resumes even before the humans will read them. They are searching for certain jargon, firms, and job titles to determine if specific, requisite skills and experience are there. If you have those skills be sure to use the exact names of each. If you don't know what I'm talking about you probably don't have any of the meat the robots are searching for.

One more thought.

Nearly everyone thinks she is a resume expert. So the more people who see your resume, the more likely they will make you nuts. My advice: Find just one person or expert and trust her advice. If some other well-meaning soul tells you to change your font, bullet points, interests, objective, date format, paper stock, etc., first check with your personal resume guru.

12

Make Contact with a Zig and a Zag.

Back in the 1990s, when I was still shoveling coal at TBWA/Chiat/Day, there was a fashionable movement in business to seek new ideas by approaching problems from a different perspective. Unsurprisingly, a catchphrase was created that lingers, maybe even prospers in some circles, to this day. It's called "Thinking outside the box."

While people who thought of themselves as unconventional thinkers had been doing this for a living for many dog years (think: The Long Island Expressway is packed; I think I'll try Grand Central Parkway) the opportunity of thinking outside the box gave people who didn't think of themselves as "creative" permission to try it out.

Thinking outside the box meant freedom; to suspend rules, take off your shoes, challenge assumptions and minimize negativity for engaging in all those activities.

Thinking outside the box began as a movement but evolved into the silly. Customers who shopped at Sears, the bastion of the rough, tools and tires – were encouraged to consider the "Softer Side Of Sears":

Chapter 12.

clothing, towels, and pillows to transform Sears into what, JCPenney?

We tried to determine if there really was a difference between left and right feet so people could wear shoes on either foot.

Do pickles have to come in a jar? What about pickle socks?

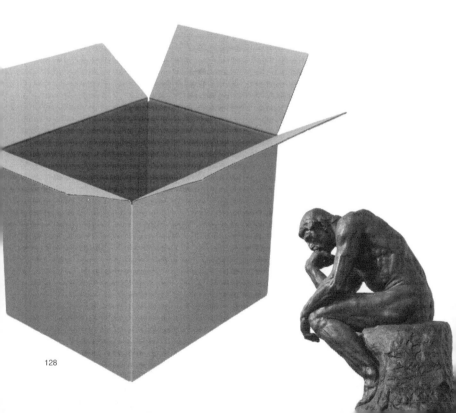

Along about then I had had enough. Since nearly everyone was now thinking outside the box, I decided it was a good time to get back into the box. I could have some peace, and there was carpeting.

There's actually a serious lesson here. It's referred to as zigging and zagging. It simply means to choose a direction that everyone else isn't going, to avoid the crowds, traffic, and particularly, competition. You remember: This book is about getting ahead of 90% of your competition.

Yes, thinking outside the box was alluring until it became just the rush hour we were trying to avoid in the first place. Yes, I'm being metaphorical: One can still think differently inside the box.

Because it's not about the box, it's about you.

A concrete example of zigging.

As recently as the 1980s, job applicants actually picked up the phone and called executives to introduce themselves. We were even a little sly, calling very early in the day when they arrived, or at the end of the day, to avoid having the secretary pick up the phone and screen the caller. Then Caller ID and voicemail became common and execs could screen their own calls. The job hunter could just hang up or leave a message, preferably, not several messages.

In the 1990s the secretary position largely disappeared. According to The New York Times, nearly two million clerical positions were eliminated between 1960-2000. (Think of all those Mad Men secretaries out of work.) Executives went back to answering their own phones unless they were at the highest end of the company's food chain, and still had a live person screening their calls, allowing in important clients.

In the 2000s, email largely replaced the phone as the

single point of contact. In the beginning when it was still somewhat novel, such execs would read their email, even from strangers. Problems emerged. First, the sheer level of email became overwhelming. People would brag, "I get 500 emails a day." Most of it would be unsolicited: Ads, pleas, and people they didn't want to hear from.

Then it became dangerous. Nigerian princes who left you money, just click here; friends' accounts that had been hacked, requesting funds transmitted to Thailand; make-believe, lookalike "Citibank" messages, requesting you contact them through a link. When people are afraid, they aren't opening the door to strangers. And worst of all, they are afraid of viruses taking over their computers, stealing their information.

In a few short years, what had been the primary method of reaching out to firms has become nearly a closed road. Many execs use 'white lists," approved senders who get their mail delivered. And if you haven't met, you're hardly approved.

But like all rules there are exceptions, of course. Which means you can still try sending email to prospects and see how it works for you. If your response rate is zero the opened mail rate probably was zero, too.

What can you do to get noticed?

Write a real letter. On real paper. Send it through the real mail. With a real stamp.

The real letter is your well-crafted, intriguing, cover letter. The huge stack of postal mail arriving each day has shrunk dramatically. There are still magazines, journals, and some bills. But very little envelope mail; that is, those white envelopes that contain letters. They get noticed, they get opened, and they get read. You can either hand-write or type the addressee. Include a return address. Don't try to create a mystery on the envelope regarding the identity of the sender.

Jennifer Cotten
123 Broad Street
Boomtown, UT 12345

John Masters

Pick up the phone.

Many execs still pick up their office phone when at their desks. So you have to be prepared if this actually happens. Which means a very short, memorized script to get to the next stage, the meeting. Most people will give you a chance to speak unless they'd been expecting an important call and you snuck through. Even then, you can ask if you can call back at a better time. Don't loiter if she insists she has to go. Here's a sample way to handle someone who doesn't have to hang up right away.

> *"Hello, Mr. Coburn, I'm Neal Newman. I understand you're in charge of the Hershey's account. [Pause} I'm doing some career fact-finding and wondered if you could spare 15 minutes of your schedule sometime this month. I won't waste your time, either, because people say I'm an interesting person, too."*

You communicate that you know what he does, what you want, how long it will take, and why you are calling. All in 15 seconds!

Now, even 15 minutes can be a big investment on his part. He'll likely ask for you to elaborate what you just said or to send him some additional info like your resume or work samples.

Therefore you have to be prepared to talk more. Why Hershey's? What are you currently doing? Why are you interesting? This requires preparation so you don't go faint when someone answers the phone.

Send a fax.

Like the U.S. mail, this is another method of walking around the fence. Firms receive faxes two ways. The old-fashioned way is the fax machine that someone monitors. Between blast faxes of restaurant menus and ink cartridge specials, some faxes are still letters or other important documents, hand-delivered to the recipient. The new-fashioned way involves the office's technology. Faxes are converted to emails and arrive in the recipient's email box. But the difference is it says, "Fax" so the reader knows it's safe. And it's unusual.

Contact through LinkedIn.

Actually, this is more of a zig (everyone's doing it) versus a zag (very few are doing it). But it still works much of the time, because it demonstrates you know how to use LinkedIn, because your recipient's mailbox is probably less full, and, importantly, because your message is safe for the receiver, as LinkedIn doesn't allow links to be included inside messages. Also, if you're willing to invest $25/month you can send "InMail" which doesn't require a third party to introduce you. (NB: As of this writing, Spring 2014)

I have to warn you though, there are some things you just shouldn't do because they are mostly self-defeating: They will take you out of the game before it even begins.

This seems like a good time to also warn against employing techniques that will either reduce your chances of getting to the interview stage or eliminate them all together.

Don't.

Don't just show up at the office without an appointment.

This may have worked in black and white movies in the 1940s, but it doesn't work today. Your unexpected arrival will just make everyone angry and get you put on the "crazy" list at that office.

Don't send homemade cakes.

Or any treats you think may sweeten up the target. They will probably just get tossed along with your credentials.

Don't telephone incessantly.

Some smart people will say, "Call every day." This will rarely work unless 1) you leave a different, creative message each day, 2) the person doesn't think you're stalking her, and 3) you're very lucky.

Don't get discouraged.

Sometimes the first letter or call just doesn't get through the clutter. Send or call again. Feel free to acknowledge you've been trying. My personal favorite line is: "Since life is a frequency medium I'm writing again." You're welcome to use it.

Finally, fashions and rules change. Today's zig is tomorrow's zag. And if you think of a method that works for you then by all means, use it. And be sure to let me know.

13

How to Interview Like George Clooney.

When I was a smart-ass young person, I would arrive at the interview with my neatly folded resume and my ability to answer questions on the fly. My two-edged sword was my ability to think fast on my feet and my total lack of preparation for the interview. Preparation seemed like cheating. But the simple truth is I was lazy and uninformed. Now I am neither, and I won't let you be either.

I have come to understand that interviews are performances that require preparation and rehearsal until they become second nature. Many people have a fear of public speaking, but interviews are really much tougher and typically have more at stake than making a prepared speech to a willing audience. Let me smooth the interviewing road, enabling you to be more confident and better prepared.

The soul of the interviewer.

Most interviewers don't try to scare the hell out of you. Or try to make you feel like a puppy that just pooped on the carpet. Or spend thirty minutes talking about themselves as opposed to getting to know you. But these people exist and always will.

Most interviewers have an agenda. They have a method that works for them to determine very quickly if you've got the right stuff or you don't. Professionals tell me they know within five minutes if you're suitable. I think they exaggerate: they know in two minutes.

They do this through eye contact. Are you looking at them while speaking, or are you looking up, down, and around?

They observe your posture. Are you sitting up straight, leaning slightly forward, in deference and in interest?

They examine your clothes. Are you properly dressed for the meeting? Which means, no matter how casual you know the office dress code to be, you always dress above it. If you've been smoking tobacco they will smell it on your clothes. And if they don't like smokers, they won't like you.

They set little traps. By asking "little" questions to see if you talk yourselves past the answer and say

things you shouldn't. Which means: Once you've answered the question stop talking.

They try to remember why they agreed to meet you.
Don't laugh. Or cry. Most execs now do the work of 1.5 people versus a decade ago. They are juggling, and sometimes the balls drop.

They wonder if you will fit into the organization.
Its culture, personality, and whether you're someone he can imagine spending any time with.

They ask their killer question. Of course it varies from person to person but I will tell you in the next chapter what it is with 95% certainty so you're prepared.

You look at this list and wonder how anyone ever gets hired, let alone you.

Let's get started.

I hesitate to tell you the little stuff because I don't want to patronize you, but let's just get this out of the way. It's the little stuff you can control, so read carefully.

Arrive ten minutes before the appointment. That means at the reception area or office door. Not the building lobby where you first may have to be announced and pass through security, wait for the elevator, or be shepherded by a company employee.

Bring three copies of your resume and cover letter. Always. Yes, they probably have a copy somewhere, but it's not their job to look for it.

Go to the restroom. Look in the mirror, if only to make sure you weren't attacked by a pigeon on the walk over. And check to see if you have any spinach caught between teeth, even if you don't eat spinach.

Return to reception. Place a relaxed look on your face. Tell yourself a joke. Meditate. Imagine you're on a beach (assuming you like the beach).

Don't. Chew gum. Carry a beverage. Eat a banana. Or do any personal housekeeping like comb, file, or scratch. I once lost a job I was on the verge of being offered because I let down my guard, crossed my leg, and lit a cigarette. (This was in the 1970s when people still smoked in offices.) The smoking wasn't the problem as much as I made myself too comfortable. My friend Ingram reminds me of this incident at least twice a year.

Here comes the good news: You belong here. You've earned the interview. You're not a fake. You just have to be the person who wrote that great letter.

If the interviewer doesn't recall your Brand, feel free to mention it early.

"I'm the Scottish dancer."
"I'm the guy who chases whales."
"I'm the person who dreams about work."

Now it's time to get to business.

If you believe there's a specific job you're interviewing

for then your assignment is a little easier.

Sometimes you won't even know until the interviewer first assesses you. You just have to frame your performance around two criteria:

1. **You can do the job**. This means you have the skill set, transferable experience, or mind-set and attitude to learn and adapt.

2. **You want the job.** Just like you want to be loved, the company wants to be loved, too. Companies need to believe you're not just passionate about you but passionate about them, so you should offer reasons why you believe.

It's just that simple. Really.

If you're not interviewing for a specific job or department, it's still necessary to salute the company flag.

Earlier I spoke about the absolute need to prepare for the performance aspect of the meeting. Here's a tip

I learned from one of my daughter's friends at Yale, someone who is also an accomplished actress.

After you memorize key phrases to the likely interview questions – they appear in the next chapter – don't recite them like you memorized The Gettysburg Address in eighth grade.

Rather, pause here and there; look up as if you're thinking of what to say next, even though you know exactly what you plan to say. Bite your lip (but not too hard as to bleed).

These gestures will make your answers look less canned and more spontaneous. You can also mutter an occasional *"Umm."*

This isn't cheating: it's just smart interviewing. Why? Because the interviewer is always in the "power position."

He knows what questions he's going to ask. These tips help you play defense a little better in order to reduce the gap between interviewer and interviewee.

President Clinton's trademark bite-the-lip tactic.

14

Ten Questions You Must Be Ready to Answer.

Job interviewing hasn't changed very much in the past 40 years, my timeframe as interviewee, interviewer and observer of this mating ritual. It shouldn't surprise that as a practice, we interviewers ask pretty much the same often irritating and inane questions we were asked in your position. Why? I believe there are three reasons:

First, we believe these answers will help us decide if you've got the right stuff.

Second, we have the "power," to ask pretty much whatever we want. Sometimes this just leaks into idle curiosity.

Third, we want to give you a chance to impress or distress by requiring you to think on your feet with questions you haven't prepared.

Which explains why you need to prepare mental answers to all these questions, prior to the interviews.

10 questions:

1. Tell me about yourself.

2. What is your biggest success or what are you most proud of to date?

3. What is your biggest weakness?

4. Where do you want to be five years from now?

5. Who is your most important influencer?

6. Why did you study (particular major)?

7. Why do you want to work in this industry?

8. Why do you want to work here?

9. Tell me about a failure or obstacle you overcame.

10. What would you do if....?

Why should we hire you?

1. Tell me about yourself.

You're probably thinking, "Yeech, I hate this question." It is both the most frequently asked question and typically it's the leadoff, just when you are the most vulnerable. Lucky you have already figured out your Brand and have crafted your story around it. So, rather then recite a rigid chronological autobiography or random highlights, you don't have to invent here:

> *"I'm happy to. As I wrote in my letter, I'm a Scottish dancer. I was attracted to it when I was a teen because it required intense focus to learn all the moves, I welcomed the competition – particularly when I won; I found it both very challenging and fun, though more the former than the latter; and I got to meet a lot of other great people."*

This 24-second answer says so much more than a predilection toward an unusual hobby: your ability to focus, your enjoyment of competition and winning, your recognition that challenges can also be fun, and that you're a people person (without using that odious phrase). It has a beginning, a middle, and an ending, all in less time than watching a McDonald's ad.

2. What is your biggest success or what are you most proud of to date?

They are looking for initiative, teamwork, and leadership examples such as projects that required cooperation, selflessness, where you aren't the hero but helped other people perform better. Avoid: Little League home runs, drinking contests, and any acts of stupidity masked as bravery.

3. What is your biggest weakness?

This is a real trap. You aren't talking to your therapist or significant other. The best way to frame this answer is to place a weakness in a strength box. For example, "I tend to take my job too seriously and think about it even when I'm not at work." Most companies want you to obsess about your job, particularly in this 24/7 connectivity phase we are in, so a work-too-hard answer resonates.

4. Where do you want to be five years from now?

I know what you're thinking: Not in this chair answering these questions. And probably not in this company either. Good thing he can't read your mind. Most firms need to believe you want to work there until you drop, but they know that's not the case. What you need to articulate, however, is that once you get this job you will work your butt off. Explain it's likely the job will present opportunities you may not foresee, today. You may return to school to get an advanced degree. Or the company may diversify and want you to learn a new business offering.
(This demonstrates your ability to plan ahead, which is the whole point of the question.)

For instance, you're applying for a job as a paralegal in a law firm. You can envision learning the ropes for two years, and then going to law school, finally to return to the firm as an associate!

5. Who is your most important influencer?

It's rarely a bad idea to mention a parent, as it's a good bet you're speaking to one. Also, teachers, coaches and community leaders. Be prepared to explain why: Say, the person serves as a role model for honesty, stick-to-it-ness, and treats everyone with respect, etc. (While, in practice, most people do not treat everyone with respect, they like to know there are some people out there who do.) Avoid: Ephemeral pop stars like Justin Bieber and people who are famous just for being famous. Let that stay your secret.

6. Why did you study (particular major)?

As you know all too well, everyone you know didn't study pre-med; plan to get an MBA; or study computer science. But you have nothing to apologize for – really! – for studying French, the Classics, Philosophy, Psychology, and all the liberal arts and humanities majors available. Why? College is a time to explore and to learn how to learn (that phrase is a winner). Don't allow your Philosophy degree to let others mock you for "wanting to be a philosopher." Rather, philosophy and other fields enabled you to understand complex problems, interpret peoples' motivations, and be sensitive to different cultures. These and other skills will make you successful at work, too.

7. Why do you want to work in this industry?

This is the most rational question you're likely to be asked, so you need to have your most rational answer. You might be amazed to hear that applicants to advertising agencies still say, *"I like to watch TV, especially the ads."* If this is you, it's a thought better kept to yourself. Instead, consider this example, one that is thought out:

> *"Advertising is inescapable. We are exposed to thousands of ads daily. Obviously, most of them are unsuccessful. This is a puzzle. I want to figure out how to participate in making ads work better without driving customers crazy."*

This is just one way of skinning the cat. It demonstrates a little knowledge and a lot of curiosity. All you need to do is pick a problem of the industry you're considering and, if true, make it your area of interest.

Simple, huh?

8. Why do you want to work here?

You've done your research on the Web. You've read the company website. You've Googled any published articles about it. If you have a friend there you've asked for any inside poop. You've let all this simmer in your mind so as to have an understanding of how the company describes itself and how the universe describes it. Now it's time to transform this knowledge into informed opinions. This has to go beyond the superficial comments such as

> *'I like the culture.*
> *I admire the work.*
> *You serve great coffee."*

Nearly every firm has an emphasis, a specialty, and its own Brand. They don't try to be everything to all people. Examine it. Assess it. Don't be afraid to voice an opinion based on knowledge gained as an outsider. You will demonstrate both the research you did and the thinking it prompted.

9. Tell me about a failure or obstacle you overcame.

As most of us don't walk the earth thinking about our ugly past, this is truly an opportunity to take a long pause before answering the question. Hmmm... Let me check my Rolodex for personal failures. On the extreme side, perhaps you immigrated to the USA without speaking English or having any friends, or you suffered a childhood illness, or experienced a severe financial reversal in your family that caused you to move or substantially reduce your lifestyle. How did you cope?

More likely, you were on a team, or in a play, or were in an organization where you were bottom banana and had to work your way up through practice, practice, and practice. Or maybe you realized you weren't going to be a good baseball player or flautist, and then chose another path.

My travail: As a junior in high school I was failing chemistry much of the year. I didn't really care, as while I didn't know a lot about my future I did know I wasn't going to become a chemist. My guidance counselor, Miss Lomench, reminded me colleges might not see it my way. My chemistry teacher, Mr. Goldenberg, even bet me $5.00 (a tidy sum in 1968) that I would fail the Regents exam. Ah, motivation! I bought the review book and essentially learned the year's course in a week of after-school studying. I earned an 85 on the exam. I recommend, however, you come up with your own bridge to success.

10. What would you do if….?

Remember, they can ask any question they want, because they sit on the other side of the desk. The "What if?" question may be the most useless of all, but that's probably not the best response. It usually assumes you've been on the job (or had a similar job) and have to react to a difficult employee or client or boss.

Plus you probably can't ask any questions that give you any more context to the hypothetical.

This is probably a good time to say something packaged that best encompasses how you approach all problems. For instance, "I would gather the facts as best I could; determine if there were any precedents to guide me; speak to a superior who isn't my boss (if my boss is somehow involved); and then come to a conclusion, quickly, but not hastily." In other words, don't agree to shoot the horse.

OK, imagine you have now survived the questions that separate the winners from the losers. But you realize they haven't asked the question that touches on something critical you wanted to say. Perhaps they didn't ask. Or you forgot. Or you couldn't squeeze it in. And perhaps it was the most important question of all:

Why should we hire you?

Remember this is the sum of

Why **you** can do the job
+ Why **you** want the job

You get the job!

The interviewer may simply ask if you have any other thoughts. More likely, you will have to volunteer, "I do have some final thoughts."

Since you have crafted three or four sentences that build on your Brand, and you understand the skills and attributes the job requires, intertwined with your expressed love of the firm, you are ready for the proposal. This mating game is exactly like a marriage, and you've arrived at the altar!

Here's an example:

> *"When I became a Scottish dancer I just thought I liked dancing. I didn't know yet I was also attracted to the concentration, competition, and achievement it required. Of course I've matured since I was 13, so when I get this job I will develop the additional skills necessary to be personally successful but importantly, quickly contribute to the firm's success, too. I will be successful here."*

Wow, this a confident statement from a job applicant, but still not over the top. She actually slips in the phrase, "When I get this job…" demonstrating optimism and confidence, she visualizes the victory. We can see her smile as she speaks these words.

The closing speech also emphasizes the job isn't about making her marketable. It's about developing skills to help the firm. And without simply saying, "I want to work here," she means, I want to work here! Though I wouldn't fault her for saying that, too!

I do... want to work here.

15

After You Leave the Building.

Wow. You just survived and probably thrived in that interview. Sure, you will think of questions you could have answered more confidently, more precisely, and more succinctly. But you will improve with practice. You've left the rehearsals and are performing now to a live audience. What's next?

More executives to meet.

Unless you've met the CEO and the job is working for her, you very likely will have to meet others in the organization, especially if there is a particular position you are being considered for. This can occur on the same day or, more likely, over several days or even weeks. I thought it was unusual when I got my job at TBWA/Chiat/Day that I returned seven different times to meet nine different people over the course of sixty days. (And more than once, I thought I blew it.) Each time I was given the name of the next exec I had to meet and told to contact him to arrange the appointment. I felt like a playing piece working my way around the Monopoly board. This can happen to you, too.

At these subsequent meetings, it's very easy to make a big mistake.

You might believe the interviewers speak to each other about you, or because you're asked the same or similar questions, you become bored with your thought out answers, so you change them. In a word, **DON'T!**

Don't veer from your story, and don't assume these people talk about you.

These people are doing a thousand different things at work, and seeing you is just one item on their to-do list. This doesn't mean they don't enjoy meeting you. It does mean they're not thinking about you on the train home.

So you have to be certain to make the same great impression on everyone. Don't take your foot off the gas.

And when they do meet their colleagues and get around to talking about your candidacy, it's often in very quick and emotional terms such as,

*"Yeah I liked her. She had grit.
We need more people with grit"*

"No, he's not a fit here."

"No, I don't think he needs this job."

"She made me laugh during a tough day."

*"I can see her bopping around here.
She's an 'up' person."*

And you thought the company gathers everyone together in a conference room with a pile of resumes to review. Sure, that happens very occasionally. But most people in firms are just too busy to have those meetings. Maybe, an HR person chases everyone down for a fast opinion. Or your potential boss sends an internal email asking, "What did you think of Jennifer Cotten, the Scottish dancer?

A "test" assignment.

It's not uncommon to be asked to complete an assignment that measures your suitability for the job. It can be totally fabricated, or it may be a current project that's on the executive's mind and he's looking to pick your brain. (This is not the same as showing work samples from a previous job or college course. This is new work.)

The assignment may test your research, writing, analytic, or creative skills. Maybe, all four.

If you're at all unclear what they need, ask questions! To ease the pressure somewhat, you may be told, no hurry, take your time, get it to me when you can.

That is a trick!

Because in addition to testing your writing skills, they are likely testing your level of interest in the position and your ability to interpret what he's actually saying.

What he's really saying:

GET THIS TO ME AS FAST AS YOU CAN, AS BEST AS YOU CAN. I DON'T WANT TO THINK YOU WERE BUSY DOING SOMETHING ELSE AND THIS WASN'T IMPORTANT. I KNOW I SAID TAKE YOUR TIME, BUT THAT'S NOT WHAT I MEANT!

I know you want to know how fast is fast. Turn it around in 24 – 48 hours. And make it great. This will probably be the difference of getting the job and not.

Thank You notes.

Yes, you need to write them to everyone you meet. They can be handwritten or emailed. So you want to get a business card from everyone so you have their contact info and, more importantly, the correct spelling of their name. (Nothing, absolutely nothing, kills your job prospects as quickly or completely as misspelling a person's name.)

What should it say? In addition to the standard, *"It was great meeting you; thanks for your time; look forward to next steps"* boilerplate, you have an opportunity to advance your candidacy.

You want to build on a slice of the conversation with that individual. It could be about his role in the firm. Or a project he's working on. Or even something in the industry or in the news.
And by build, I mean to **add** something to the conversation, not just **repeat** what was said.
For example:

BRENDA SNOOT

Dear Mr. Zarchy,

I really appreciate your generous time yesterday.

Your description of the business development role in the firm clarified my understanding of the 24/7 nature of the job.

Perhaps I'm naïve, but my father taught me relentlessness and dedication are the bedrocks of success. You've demonstrated them in your career and I will in mine.

Sincerely,

Brenda Snoot

Brenda Snoot

Jennifer Cotten

Dear Mr. Erdman,

I had another thought about the conversation we had yesterday regarding active apparel.
I've noticed at my gym women wear a variety of fashionable workout wear. The shoes are in pink, green, orange and other neon colors. Perhaps women want to be encouraged to have several pairs of exercise shoes, just as we have several fashionable watches.

Thanks again for your generous time; I'm ready for any next steps in the hiring process.

Best,

Jennifer Cotten

Jennifer Cotten

The first note hammered Brenda's work ethic, passed down from her Dad, and mirrored Mr. Zarchy's philosophy.

The second note picked up on a conversation Jennifer had with Mr. Erdman but importantly built on the conversation instead of merely parroting it.

Both notes are short, pointed, and cliché free.

Don't have a big mouth.

When interviewing and under consideration for a job, don't blab about it to your friends. Of course I'm not suggesting this is bad luck (though you never know). The real reason is you don't want to create any unnecessary, additional competition for "your" job. Sure, your close friends aren't going to apply to a firm where you're in process or pending. (Your life isn't an episode of "*Girls*".)

But…they may inadvertently mention it to their friends, people who don't know you and have no loyalty to you… and they may contact that company. So keep quiet until you have the job or are certain you don't.

What if there is no immediate job?

Remember, you contacted the firm with no strings attached. Just because you are interested in working at MTV today doesn't mean they have a suitable position today. Firms meet applicants for "futures": the possibility there will be a need. Sometimes there is a current need the interviewer will choose to reveal in the interview. Or not, if he doesn't think you're right upon speaking with you. Which means you will have interviews that don't lead to immediate jobs. But you are networking and honing your interviewing skills.

When it's clear you're in a meeting that doesn't have an immediate opening you want to:

Not show your disappointment.

Ask if there are other people in the organization you could meet.

Ask if he knows people in other companies who he recommends meeting. Good executives are always looking for the next generation of talent.

Good people want to help you get started. It's in their genes.

Ask how frequently you should follow-up.
A month? Two months? And keep track.
Be systematic. Create an Excel chart of contacts and next steps.

Feel good about your progress. Remember, you're not looking for jobs for 100 people. You're looking for a job for just one person. **You.**

Chapter 15.

16

We Want You!

Finally, you hear the magic words:

"We want to hire you. When can you start?"

But before you pop the champagne cork there may be a few obstacles that need to be hurdled.

References.

Firms can afford to be more careful these days. And they are. Perhaps you included a few business, educational, or personal references on your resume. Even if you did, it's necessary to have a separate sheet of references that include all critical contact information: Name, Title, Company, Business address, email, and phone. This includes personal references as well.

You now need to alert everyone of a pending reference check. Give them details of the company and position so they can tailor their reference to the position. Ask them to let you know when they're contacted. When I'm contacted for a reference, I take it very seriously and take special pride in helping applicants secure the job. My batting average reflects it: 1.000.

Money.

Here's a generalization: Most first jobs offer the candidate limited leverage on salary negotiation. Firms have guidelines and a history for these positions. And while you're probably exhilarated about the offer you can still try to improve it without jeopardizing anything. Simply ask if there is a salary range for the job you're offered and where your number sits. Once you know if there is any wiggle room you can just ask if the offer can rise to the upper range. I estimate it can nearly half the time. Either way it's fair to ask when the performance review is scheduled.

Start date.

Since you don't want to look like a dummy after you got this far, you have to plan ahead. You need to provide adequate (1-2 weeks) notice if you have a current job or internship or any responsibility. You also need to plan: If you're going to an out-of-town wedding or planned a vacation, now is the time to tell them. The last thing you want to do is start a job and say, "Oh, do you mind if I take next week off?" Yes, they mind. A lot.

Benefits.

You probably didn't ask about them during the interview process, and that speaks to your good sense. Now is a fine time to ask. The HR department is skilled at explaining them. Benefits including vacation, medical/dental, 401K, etc. are rarely negotiable for entry-level positions.

Confirmation letter.

Some job candidates hallucinate they've been offered the job. These people request a confirmation letter or email that includes title, salary, start date, and often, the duties. This is not a legal document but it is good to show nervous parents. If you are one of those people, by all means, ask. Firms rarely refuse but also can be slow in sending them out. If you don't need one, so much the better.

17

Days One, Two, Three.

I have a saying about the first day on a job: *"It's good to get to Day 1, even better to get to Day 2."*

First days can be exhilarating, scary, humbling, and bewildering. You meet many people (all those names to learn!); get a sense about doing your job versus hearing a job description; and discover there often is free food for the taking. And everyone knows, free food tastes better. After living and observing many First Days I'll share my advice. Ignore at your peril.

Hit the ground running.

This is an expression parachutists use to describe what they do after jumping out of airplanes. The running prevents hard landings, reducing broken legs. You want to hit the ground running as someone starting a new job, in motion, visible and dynamic. You want colleagues and bosses to know you're there by words and deeds. Sure, you have to learn before offering informed opinions, but don't be a mouse, squeaking around, trying not to be noticed. Just as in interviews, people will form opinions about you in a hurry.

Leave your cocoon.

Shortly after meeting your immediate colleagues or team or department, don't be afraid to see what else is happening in your company. I'm not suggesting you knock on office doors (if there still are any), but wander and sniff. Most offices have open floor plans making people more accessible. Introduce yourself. Get known. See, an amazing thing has happened upon your hiring. You are no longer an outsider, escorted around the building. You are an insider, and the difference is enormous. You get to learn how your firm actually works, see who does what, and make valuable contacts for the future.

Volunteer.

Naturally you have much to learn about your new job. You want to be perfect, but that's just not going to happen. New tasks take longer, and roles are sometimes fuzzy (do I have to change the printer ink?). You're trying to distinguish between who is there to help you and who is trying to kill you. Unfortunately, there is still at least one asshole in every firm, and that is never going to change. But even with your heavy workload, find time to volunteer when someone is needed.

It may be a dirty job no one else wants to do. It may mean hopping on a train to another city to deliver a presentation. It may mean an opportunity to demonstrate your team-at-all-costs approach and impress other "bosses" you haven't met.
I'm not suggesting doing anything illegal, immoral, or dangerous. But you'll know it when it comes.
And, shock, it might even be fun.

What time should you go home?

Before you can go home you first have to arrive. Is it really necessary to say it's critical – particularly in the beginning – to arrive on time? Better, arrive 15-30 minutes early. Don't be one of those subway blamers: "My train was late." It's just so wimpy weary. A good rule of thumb states junior employees are the last to leave the building. Of course that assumes they actually have legitimate work to do. It's rarely a bad idea to be sure your boss goes home first.
But if you're left with absolutely nothing to do but overcome Candy Crush Level 130 and your boss is still working, ask her if there's anything else you can

do that day. Don't just sneak out thinking your exit goes unnoticed. Someone is always watching.

Stay off your smartphone.

And put it out of sight. You are now on company time. All personal calls, texts, and social media updates must only be done when you're on a break, at lunch, and away from your desk. If you're in a meeting and see other employees with their phones on the table, you still shouldn't do it. Plus, there's a different rule for bosses: They can do whatever they want.

Beer.

Many firms with a high density of young people who have apartments the size of PortaPotties encourage their employees to work well into the evening rather than rushing home. They may offer weekly or monthly beer and chips nights as both a lubrication and reward. Just try to remember you're still in the office (and not at a fraternity party). Don't overdo it, don't oversay it, and don't overmess it.

Under promise, over deliver.

Dotted-line bosses.

It's fairly typical to have more than one "boss" when you start out. It becomes clear that practically everyone is atop you on the corporate totem pole, even if they don't wear stripes on their shoulders or possess a certain number of feathers in their headdresses.

You learn that even if you don't report to someone directly, that person may have influence over your future. You want to impress everyone. One way to do this, is to not disappoint by missing a deadline you weren't even aware of. So when someone, anyone, asks you to do something, regardless how small, always ask when he needs it. Because you don't know what they're thinking and they probably don't know what else you're doing, you have to be clear, so you don't disappoint. Don't make crazy promises you can't keep. And don't say you'll do the best you can. That is assumed. Remember: This isn't high school, this is business.

Seek feedback.

We all want positive reinforcement. We all need to get progress reports so we don't paint false pictures in our minds that we are stars when we aren't. Most firms conduct periodic performance reviews. But somewhere between being screamed at and praised is that vast middle ocean of, "How am I doing?" Feel free to ask, just not every day.

18

Next.

I'm often asked how long you need to stay before leaving for your next job. There's actually a very simple and clear answer: One year. Not three months, not six months, but a full twelve-month year.

Of course this assumes you've decided this industry, firm, and job aren't right for you. Let's hope not. But life isn't perfect and you have earned the right to be happy and figure out what's next.

There are steps to take while inside this job to determine if you should stick around beyond the first year.

Find a mentor.

This may be your boss or your boss' boss or someone in an entirely different department who takes an interest in your success and appreciates your talents and potential outside the everyday rush of soldiering and deadlines. Also, as you meet more colleagues you'll discover some teams or groups or departments are having a lot more fun than you; conversely, some teams are having less fun.

You may have been hired by a great company and just have the bad luck of working for or with less inspiring people. Or maybe you've been assigned to a project or client that is the business equivalent of a bad sandwich, and you're the filling. Motivate yourself to do the best possible job under the circumstances, and don't walk around with a sour face.

Talk to people there who have a few years of experience; they can guide you through the rough periods. I don't recommend over-sharing with Human Resources. There is no lawyer/client privilege here requiring them to maintain confidentiality.

Don't leave this job without securing the next job.

Many companies engage in some odd and rigid thinking. They believe job candidates with current jobs are much better prospects than candidates without. They believe there may be something wrong with you if you left a job without obtaining the next job. They may not believe your reasons for leaving as they have been hardened through experience that everyone stretches the truth about exits, even though some of the best people I know have been fired at least once. As with all generalizations sometimes this one is actually correct. So don't put yourself in this jam if you don't have to.

I think that's it. But because I know I will think of more stuff to tell you and I want to hear what you learn, what you figure out on your career journey, I've set up a Facebook page. Stop by, air your thoughts, spread your ideas, and enjoy.

This coupon entitles the bearer to:

ONE FREE CAREER

Not redeemable in real life.
Coupon expires 03-04-2012.

Additional Resources.

There's seemingly no limit to job and career advice out there. Some places also worth your time:

The New York Times.

Every Friday in the Business section is a column called "Corner Office." These are interviews of CEOs and other execs conducted by Adam Bryant. They are full of personal stories, including how they search for new employees and the kinds of questions they ask. For instance, Alan Dabbiere, chairman of AirWatch, in September 2013 said: "We ask people if they feel lucky. We want people to feel lucky because the harder you work, the luckier you get. So people who work hard actually feel lucky."

The Brand Gap *by Marty Neumeier*

This is the only text I've used in my Branding course year after year. Interestingly, it's actually not written for consumers but for businesses, helping them straighten out their branding.

Mr. Money Mustache. (MrMoneyMustache.com)
I stumbled onto this website very recently. MMM
gives great life-advice, particularly discouraging folks
from getting too caught up in the "money chase."
He might just let you know you already could be
successful without even knowing it! I've yet to read a
false note in anything he says.

Acknowledgements.

Book designer and art director, *Juergen Dahlen*.
I had to convince him to join the team, because even
after 30 years, he likes to play hard to get.

Brainy guy, *Bob Ingram*. I realized as I was writing, he
taught me much of what I know in this department,
four decades back.

My NYU student team of Hansel & Gretel:
Sander Aaron Siegel & *Katharine Boris*.
Simultaneously, they are both young and old for their
age.

Isabel, my wife. Always my inspiration,
always my best critic.

*See, when you have the right tools,
looking for a job is like finding a
needle in a haystack.*

12517459R00115

Made in the USA
San Bernardino, CA
22 June 2014